Written by Laurence Ottenheimer
Illustrated by Michelle Nikly

Specialist adviser:
Embassy of Japan
Katsuko Verkhovskoy and Yoshie Shigematsu

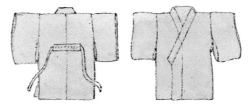

First U.S. Publication 1988 by
Young Discovery Library
217 Main St. • Ossining, NY 10562

ISBN 0-944589-11-1
©*Editions Gallimard 1984*
Translated by Ann M. TenEyck
English text ©by Young Discovery Library.
Thanks to Irene Coleman Dillon

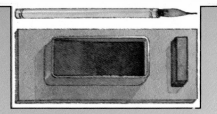

Japan:
Land of Samurai
and Robots

Where does the sun rise first..?

YOUNG DISCOVERY LIBRARY

The Japanese flag is the symbol of Japan's other name: Land of the Rising Sun.

Japan is in Asia, very far from here. It is a chain of 1,042 islands!

It is a very small country compared to its neighbors China and Russia.

When children in Chicago are having lunch, the Japanese are still asleep.

We do not live in the same time zone

Japanese money is the yen.

as they do, because a great distance separates us. From Chicago it takes at least 12 hours by plane to go to Tokyo, the capital. When it is 12 o'clock noon in Chicago, it is 3 a.m. in Japan and it is already the next day.

Japanese stamp and license plate.

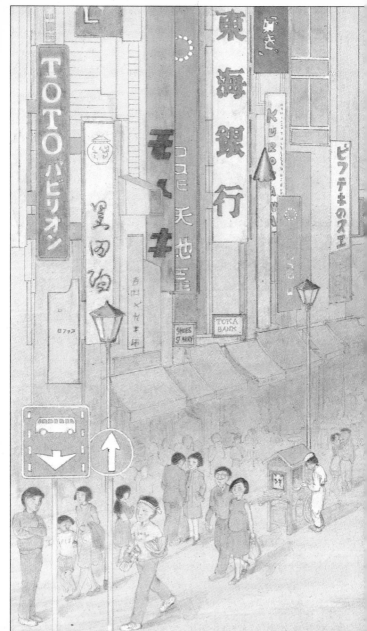

They have many earthquakes in Japan.

Many of
the people
keep a sur-
vival kit

at home, also a padded hood which
protects them from falling objects.

There are many volcanoes.

The highest is Fujiyama. Today,
among the 225 Japanese volcanoes,
60 of them can still become
active.

Tokyo and its suburbs form one of the biggest cities in Asia.

On the roofs of the apartment
buildings there are tennis courts
or mini golf courses. On the
different basement levels there
are banks, stores and restaurants.

In the subway, when
everyone is packed
in, the pusher's
job is to close
the doors.

A traditional Japanese house.

It is made of wood and built on piles in order to withstand earthquakes. The garden does not resemble an American garden. It imitates a real countryside in miniature: a pool where carp swim replaces the pond, pebbles take the place of large rocks;

a carpet of moss and clumps of fern or bamboo: the forest. The most precious trees are **bonsai**, which are specially pruned so that they grow old without getting bigger. Some of these miniature trees are over 100 years old and measure only 10 inches in height! They are very valuable.

Why do they take off their shoes when going into the house?

The floor is covered with mats of braided rush called **tatamis**. In order not to dirty them, they walk on them in socks. In the house there are no doors but

sliding screens with small squares made out of rice paper. When they are dirty or torn, they are replaced. In the living room, children are not allowed to approach or play too near the **tokonama:** a little sacred alcove decorated with a pretty painting and a bouquet

In the past when they changed the tatami mats, it was a great event for everyone in the neighborhood!

of flowers, carefully
arranged: **ikebana**.
Japanese women take
courses in order to learn
how to arrange flowers.
It is a special art!

How do they eat?
The Japanese often like to eat
their meals kneeling on cushions
around a low table.

Each person chooses what he or she
wants and takes it with chopsticks:
little cubes of vegetables, meat or
fish accompany rice. Tea stays hot
in a thermos.

To stay in shape, school children do gymnastics each morning.

Japanese school children.
The books from which they learn
their language are different from

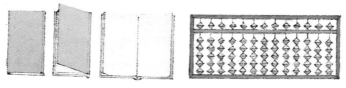

yours; their first page is your
last page and they read from right
to left. For counting they use an
abacus: the **soroban.**

They practice while
looking at, but not
touching the beads, to do
addition as fast as with a
calculator. Japanese
children also practice the
art of **origami**: by
folding paper without
either cutting or pasting
it, they make a bird, a

frog, a pig... It is necessary to make very precise movements. Japanese pupils work many hours. When class finishes, they stay at school for a music lesson or a baseball game. Then many of them go to another school to take additional courses to improve and get ahead.

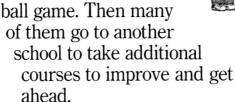

The students have much less vacation than you: one month in the summer, fifteen days in winter and in spring. The school year starts in April.

Baseball is the sport played by most adults and Japanese children.

More and more Japanese students are learning their lessons from the computer screen.

The characters are painted with a brush in India ink.

How do they write in Japanese?

Not with the 26 letters of your alphabet, but with little designs. These are characters which represent a word or an idea. There are several hundred thousand of them and nobody knows them all.

Ki = tree
te = hand

yama = mountain
hito = man

To read well, it is necessary to learn at least 2,000 characters. In the beginning, children read and write with **Kana** which are 46 very simple signs. To learn our alphabet is also useful to them. Each year, an important calligraphy contest gives a prize to the child who writes the most beautiful poem.

The bath: a moment of relaxation.

The Japanese like to take very hot baths. They come out of the bath all red, but very relaxed. At home, as well as at the public bath, each one soaps himself and rinses off before entering the bath or the pool so the water stays clean for everyone.

The bed is rolled up and unrolled.

The **fouton**, a down mattress with a cover, is stored in a closet during the day. At night, they are spread out on the tatami mats and everyone sleeps there very comfortably!

When the fouton is put away, there is plenty of space to play in the bedroom.

How do they dress for holidays?

In a silk or cotton **kimono**, gathered at the waist by a wide belt: the **obi**. Boys tie their obi for the first time at five years of age and girls at three or seven years of age. This event is the occasion for a family celebration.

Different ways to tie an obi.

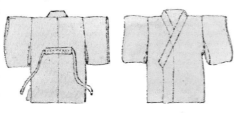

Here is a young boy's kimono. The girls' kimono has long sleeves. A married woman's kimono has short sleeves.

In March: a girls' holiday.

They put out their dolls which are not toys. The dolls represent the Emperor, the Empress, and their court.

With the kimono, they wear sandals with wooden soles and a strap for the big toe: **geta**.

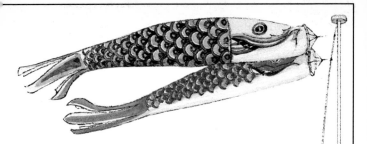

In May: a holiday for boys.
In the gardens and from the
balconies, big cloth carp float
in the wind and fill with air.
In Japan they say that these
fish are very courageous
because they swim upstream
against the current, jumping over
rocks. Mothers wish their sons to
be as brave as the carp.

**Each year the Japanese
organize giant kite flying
contests.**
The strings that hold these kites
cut like glass. Each team tries
to cut the kite strings of the
opposing team.

When they play games and sports, the
Japanese like to tie a band around their
foreheads as a sign of strength.

23

Though baseball
is the most
popular sport,
the Japanese
also practice
very old sports:

Before each contest
the judokas bow to
each other.

Judo: a contest without weapons.

It is necessary to
throw the opponent
off balance and to
immobilize him on
the ground. Judo is
good for control and
concentration.

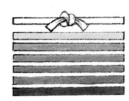

The beginner judokas wear the
white belt, the champions wear
the black belt.

Sumo: a fight between two giants who each weigh 330 lbs.

Athletes grab each other and try
to force the opponent from the
circle. The struggle lasts several
seconds!

A judo hold.

Samurai, warriors of the Middle Ages, had special ways of fighting. Today we call them **martial arts.**

Kendo: a kind of fencing. The saber

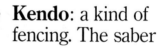

formerly used is replaced by a bamboo stick.

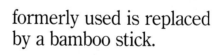

Kyudo: Japanese archery. One must have great concentration to pull the bow and aim at the target.

Karate: fighting with the hands and feet instead of weapons.

If you traveled in Japan,
you would cross

big cities, but also forests of
pine, cedar or bamboo, and immense
rice paddies.

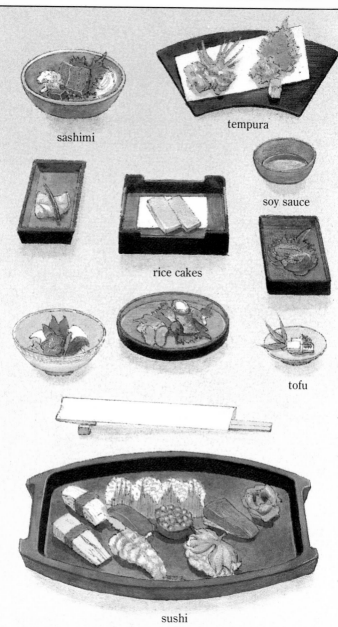

sashimi

tempura

soy sauce

rice cakes

tofu

sushi

Japan is the country where they eat the most fish.

Five times more than in the United States. Along the coasts and on all the seas of the world, the Japanese fish for dolphin, turbot, tuna, bream, shrimp, cuttlefish... They also cultivate seaweed which they dry. Like rice it is eaten with many fish dishes. The Japanese like to eat raw fish, cut into thin slices, with soy sauce. In restaurants, cooks take courses to learn how to prepare and decorate these dishes which are called **sushi.**

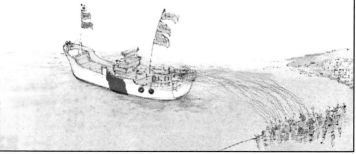

When men leave for faraway fishing, their families throw streamers at them as a sign of farewell.

In the temple gardens, Japanese tie little papers: horoscopes with written vows and wishes.

In Japan there are two religions: Shintoism and Buddhism.

The Shintos honor numerous gods. Here is a Shinto procession. The statue of the god is carried through the streets and all the people in the neighborhood follow the procession to the beat of big drums. Buddhists do not adore Buddha. They revere him as a great teacher who became godlike. The two religions teach children to be wise, good and polite to all humans and even all living things.

Statue of Buddha.

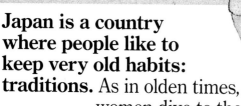

Japan is a country where people like to keep very old habits: traditions. As in olden times, women dive to the bottom of the sea without air tanks to look for oysters containing pearls. Pearls

Tea picking

make beautiful necklaces. As in the past, the Japanese wear their most beautiful kimono when they invite their friends to the tea ceremony.

But it is also a very modern country. There are seven television channels and programs

begin at 6 o'clock in the morning.
The heroes of many of your cartoons
were invented in Japan.

The Japanese sell their industrial products
throughout the entire world: cameras, video tape
recorders, calculators, watches...

In the factories, robots replace
workers. A **robot** is a kind of
automated machine that does what
people tell it to do. It is
capable of perform-
ing very precise
jobs, like the
welding of metal

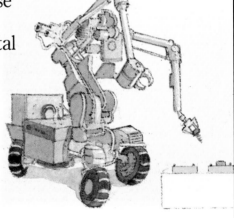

on cars. There are also robots in
the United States, but Japan is the
country which has the most.

Design inspired by
a painting of Okusai.

Japanese poets like to write **haiku**:
short three line poems. Here are
some very old ones.

Oh to have a brush
which is able to paint the plum blossoms
with their perfume!

When it melts,
ice with water
becomes friends again.

The thief
took all from me, except
the moon which was at my window.

(Miyamori)

Index